LOOKING

OUT

FROM

THE

INSIDE

THE UNITED STATES
VS. TRESSA BRANTLEY

TRESSA MITCHENER

www.tressamitchener.me

Printed in the United States of America

First Printing, 2016

ISBN: 978-1540464545

DEDICATION

God ALL the glory, honor and praise belongs to you. I would like to dedicate this book to all the hands that handle it, and that God may impart his Truth in your Spirit. That you may see his Love, Grace, and Mercy. The one and only God who is, who He says He is. Jesus Christ our Lord and Savior.

ACKNOWLEDGMENTS

I would like to thank my husband, Willie Mitchener Jr. and my best friend for your support, love, the extra push, encouraging, and believing in me for what God has assigned me to do.

I want to thank my father and my step mother Nilous and Barbara Banks for supporting me through the storm.

I want to thank my father and mother in law, Willie and Ann Mitchener Sr. for accepting me as your own, and calling me daughter from the first day. You guys are the best!

To my children, Shaquan and Deondrea Branch, thank you for cheering me on and being my biggest fans. Briona, always keep showing me that smile.

To my grandchildren, Jamir Cross, Noah Branch, and Fallyn Branch. I told my story for you so that God may get his Glory, and no one else would have to tell you since it is written. You can have my testimony of God's goodness, and believe in his covenant of Love for you.

To my brother, Nilous Banks Jr. you started the process of the fighter in me. We fought every day after school, and didn't even know why. All we knew is it was going down each day (LOL). We laugh and joke about it all the time now because we were still closely bonded after each fight, but God ignited the Spiritual (fighter) warrior in me. Thank you.

To all my family members, thank you all for having me. You all are a blessing from God to me.

To Phillip Tyler, thank you for allowing me to be me, and accepting just that "me," a woman of God that can remain faithful to Him in the workplace, and not be hindered from serving our God. Thank you for always encouraging me.

A huge thank you to Pastor Reynolds, Minister Dalphine, and Minister Barbara, thank you for staying on the path of Gods calling to bring souls into the Kingdom.

PRAYER

Lord, thank you for loving me, and choosing me. You are the Lord of Lords, King of Kings, Creator of Heaven and Earth. You are the Alpha, the Omega the beginning and the end. The first and the last, and apart from you I am nothing. Lord I ask you to enter my life and save me, set me free, deliver me, and make me whole. Lord you told me if I confess with my mouth the Lord Jesus and believe in my heart that God has raised him from the dead, I shall be saved. (Romans 10:9 NKJV) Lord I ask you to enlighten my spiritual eyes that I may see. Lord you said in your word. "If you then, being evil know how to give good gifts, to your children, how much more will your heavenly Father give the Holy Spirit to those who ask him! (Luke 11:13 NKJV) Lord I thank you fill me with your Spirit. In Jesus Name, I pray Amen.

L ooking from the outside it all looked fabulous. The nice home, luxury cars, clothes, jewelry, and of course the money. From my youth, deep within, I had been searching for something, but I really couldn't explain what it was. My brother and I never had a true sense of stability growing up. Our parents were divorced and we were back and forth between them. We really didn't like being with my mom because she had issues with alcohol and she fought all the time with her boyfriend. We still knew she loved us, and did the best that she could do, but the alcohol would get the best of her.

My mother left this boyfriend for a while, and met another one, but this ended up disastrous when he tried to molest me at the age of six. We were the only ones at home; I got away from him and ran down the street. I got to my mother's ex-boyfriend home, he didn't live far down the road, and he was furious. He went looking for this guy, but he had taken off before we got back. This incident brought my mom and her ex-boyfriend back together. He really did care for my brother and I, but he also had a drinking problem, which led to the multiple fights between the two of them. My brother and I were so tired of the fighting that we wanted to desperately stay with our dad. Our dad had a girlfriend who had no children of her own and she was amazing to us. Brenda really loved us and I appreciated everything she did for us, and for loving us the best that she could. She was truly hope to us. My brother and I learned early how to be there for one another, but Brenda showed us she was there for us too. She would take time to talk to us and take us out to eat pizza. She cooked us dinner almost every night even when she was on the second or third shift at work, she always made sure we had a cooked meal. Brenda was the best. She was the greatest sign of stability we ever had. She always wanted children, but had multiple miscarriages; eventually she did have a daughter with my dad. Brenda was interested in stability just like we were but she and my dad had differences, and she believed there was infidelity on his part.

A few years passed and her suspicions of my father got the best of her and she decided to get her own apartment, taking her daughter and moving out. Brenda was hurt because she didn't want to leave us, but she had to so that she could gain her peace. My brother and I lived with my dad for the next two years. He was hardly at home because he worked a lot, and when he was home he mainly stayed in his bedroom. We had no living room furniture because Brenda had taken it when she moved out. All my brother and I talked about was we couldn't wait to get some furniture to sit on in the living room. The woman that Brenda believed my dad was having an affair with, began to surface and come around a little here and there. Then one day my dad talked to my brother and me about her and her son moving in with us. My brother, and I were so naïve. All we thought about was finally we would have some living room furniture to sit on. It's crazy that as a child we were just trying to think of just having a place to sit in the living room, and be comfortable watching television. We had no idea that when she moved in we would hate the day we ever thought of any furniture. She was a nightmare from hell! She didn't care for us at all and it showed. We went through so much with this lady. Her son who lived with us got the best of everything. She acted as if my brother and I didn't exist when it came to spending her or my dad's money. She would cook meals and make just enough for her, my dad, and her son. She would fix their plates to assure that. When my brother and I went in the kitchen there was nothing there for us to eat. She would put notes on her furniture saying, "Do not sit". It was horrible. The very thought we had, and the only reason we wanted her there was to have furniture to sit on. She made sure that we didn't sit on hers.

One weekend her and my dad had been arguing. She never liked me and she accused my dad of being affectionate towards me in an inappropriate way. She even took out a gun in front of me. My dad was never like that towards me and I was shocked that she made such an extreme accusation. I began to dislike this woman in so many ways because she just did things so evil to break us up as a family or for my dad and I to not have a loving relationship. I returned to my mom's house. My brother and I were back and forth, but mainly my brother because I didn't even want to be around my father's girlfriend. The last incident with this woman, my brother finally ended up back at my mom's house for a while.

One day my brother and I went to my dad's house after school and the door was locked. We were ringing the doorbell and she was looking out the window at us. She just stared and wouldn't open the door so my brother grabbed a rock and broke the window. Then she came running to the door, and opened it and she was starting off with my brother. She began to fuss at him for breaking the window. She then began to call my mother out of her name with horrible words. My brother turned around to the glass cabinet where she had all her son's trophies. She seemed to idolize every piece that she had inside of it. He grabbed the entire case and tore the whole thing down. She was still running her mouth at how she was calling the police. We left and figured we would just call our dad back and let him know everything that happened and he would handle her this time for sure. Those hours waiting for him to get back home just couldn't pass by fast enough. Finally, when we figured he was home we called him.

She answered the phone, and we asked to speak to our dad. We began to tell him what happened. He stopped us and told us not to ever come to his house again unless he was home. My brother and I looked at each other with amazement. We could not believe what we were hearing. Tears began rolling down my face. My brother tried to be strong for me, but I saw the tears welling up in his eyes also. He told me it would be all right, simply because that's what he wanted to believe as bad as I did. We were 14 and 17 years old.

My dad changed the locks to his house. I had often wondered how could a father be this way and choose a woman over his children. When I was a young girl I did remember a statement my grandfather made. I heard him speaking to my grandmother and he said I do not know why my son keeps messing with that woman; she deals in "roots". I was young and had no idea what he was talking about until I got older, and learned roots were another term for witchcraft. My grandparents disliked her to the fullest extent.

I had now grown into a full blown rebellious teenager, and starting to like guys. We still loved our dad, but we were just so confused at his actions. It didn't matter if I was at my mom's house or visiting my dad. I was sneaking out the house or I was sneaking back in the house. My dad would nail my bedroom window shut, and I would take the nails right back out. It started out with just liking guys closer to my age until a twenty-one-year-old guy began to chase me. One night we were out and it was a little chilly. He took his coat off and put it around me because he saw that I was cold, and that made me feel good to see someone that seemed like they cared for me. He was known to sell drugs and had a very good connection to get them from, and a lot of it. I had just turned fifteen. His sister who was closer to my age tried to tell me not to hang out with her brother but I never thought there would come a time that I would say she was 100% correct. My mom didn't like this guy one bit. My mom did everything she could to convince me to leave him alone. She threatened him several times because of the age difference, and told him she was going to press charges on him, and call the police. He had his own place so I felt that this was a safe haven for me at the time, but little did I know this was not a good relationship.

I was also missing a ton of days from school, and they were threatening my mother to press charges on her for me missing so many days out of school because I was still considered a minor at 15. They had assigned my mom with a school counselor to try and help me to make sure I went to school, but I still was not listening, and going like I should have been. I remember my mom had come to the point where she was trying to compromise with this guy since I continued not listening to her. She told him please if she is going to keep coming to your house would you please make sure that she goes to school. She needs her education. I didn't think of it then, but now that I look back my mom didn't want me to quit school like she did, and end up with two children, and no education. He agreed with my mom saying he would make sure I went to school, but he didn't. I would still go to school when I wanted to. I was rebellious and just out of control. It was amazing because no matter how many days I missed, I was still an honor roll student. It was only the missed days that brought my grades down because I would have to do make-up work.

I wound up trying to steal something in a store and got caught. They charged and arrested me. This was not even the worst part; I became pregnant. I was 15 years old. The time came for me to go to court for the charges I was arrested for and I didn't think anything was going to happen. I figured they wouldn't send a pregnant fifteen-year-old minor away. My mother desperately wanted to do anything she could to stop me from going down this path. When it was time for me to go to court she told the judge everything she could think of to try and get me sent away, or at least get me some help. She pleaded with the judge. The school counselor also verified my attendance in school was not good. The judge sent me away to the Black Mountain Juvenile Detention facility for troubled teens in North Carolina. I was absolutely furious with my mom.

When I arrived, I met another girl there by the name of Karen. She was pregnant also and her and I hit it off really well, and talked about how we would remain friends when we got out. My mother remarried a good man for her life that had been in the military reserve. He was actually a good stepfather, trying to keep me on the right track, but I wouldn't listen. I don't think he ever knew of my childhood struggles until I was an adult and we talked. He just always knew I had incredible courage is what he called it. He reenlisted to go back in active duty. After about 6 months my mother called them and wanted to know what she needed to do to get me home because she was moving. She sent paperwork letting the detention center know she was moving out of the state, and they allowed me to get out to go with her. They would be stationed in Massachusetts. That was September 1991. I desperately wanted to do good for my mother once I got home. She did all she could do to get me home. After all she was the only one besides my aunt that made sure I had money and clothes. My cousin told the guy, whom my mother hated; that I was pregnant by what day I was coming home. When I got home I saw a car pass by, and I walked down the street with my cousin to see him. I talked to him for a few and he convinced me to just ride out with him for a while. In the car all I could think about was my mother's disappointment. We went to his mother's house because he wanted to show her how far along I was in the pregnancy, but then he refused to take me home. My mother was furious and calling because my cousin had told her that I left in the car with him. The night had passed, and my mother was calling his house. They got into an argument. I felt like I

10

had failed my mother again even after she was the only one who helped me. The guy I was pregnant by didn't even send me one dollar the entire time I was in the detention center, but as soon as I got home he was there to help me disappoint my mother again. *"For what I am doing, I do not understand. For what I will to do, that I do not practice; but what I hate, that I do" (Romans 7:15 NKJV)*

I gave birth to my first son and he was born one month premature. I was 16 years old and on welfare. My mother had moved away without me since I ended up at his house right after I got home. I think she was just at her wits end with me, but inside I wanted my mom to be happy with me. A few months after I had my son, my mom came from Massachusetts and took him back with her. His dad was abusing me physically, and I tried to get away in the middle of the night in the frigid cold with my son. In my leaving that night it caused my son to get severely ill because his lungs hadn't developed enough to breath that type of cold air. When my mom heard he was in the hospital she came and got him. This situation didn't get any better, and I wanted to have a life with my son I had just given birth to a few months prior. I got my aunt to come and get me and she gave me a one-way train ticket to Boston, Massachusetts where my mom had moved. You talking about being down in the dumps, when I got to where my mom was a few weeks later I found out I was pregnant again at 18! I gave birth to another son while living in Massachusetts. I had two children by the time I turned 19.

Now for the first time, I was thankful to my mom for doing all she could to get me sent away to Black Mountain. The facility made me attend Asheville Community College to continue my studies. If my mom had not fought so hard to get me sent away, I would have had two children and no high school diploma. Their dad managed to come to Massachusetts. He claimed if he got away to be in another state he would change. We would be happy together away from all the things we had left, and he wanted to change. When he came up there it was so much snow on the ground outside my mother couldn't let him stay outside. She still had a big heart even though she didn't like him. My mom talked to him, and she just didn't want him in her house so as soon as the snow disappeared she wanted him gone. She gave him the money to leave. I stayed in Boston for a little while and got back on my feet. I worked hard and attended a community college for some medical classes. I had a job and purchased a brand new jeep. I met a very nice gentleman with no children from Panama. His aunt and uncle brought him and his brother from Panama so that they could have a better life. I was still trying to figure out what to do with my life. Now my mother and her husband would be going to California soon, and I didn't want to go so I left and went back to North Carolina. It was like déjà vu all over again. No one knew I was coming home except my aunt. One day I went to the store and whom would I bump into but my sons' father! I was like, how could this be? His eyes locked dead into mine. He hopped in the jeep with me, and wouldn't get out the car. He wanted me to take him home since he was riding with someone else. There I was back over his house trying to leave again, but now with two kids. He would not let us leave. I was thinking by now and us not being together for this period of time that he would have changed. He had been addicted to the drugs for years and I didn't even know it. He was actually just getting by, saying he was a dealer, but he was a heavy user. I had heard many rumors, but I didn't believe it because he would never do the drugs around me. Someone called me one day and told me where he was and told me to walk in the bathroom when I got there. I did exactly what they told me and he was in the bathroom getting high. I just walked out and realized that all the rumors were true. I needed to get completely out, he was very jealous, and wanted me around him all the time. He also wanted to fight more often. Now that he knew that I knew he used drugs it got worst. He would begin to take any money I had for drug use. My children were two years old and six months. I thought by having children with him that he would change. Don't ask me why I thought that because he had numerous children everywhere.

Going through all I was going through, I hadn't spoken to my dad in a while because I felt that he chose his girlfriend over his children, but the time came when my father ended his relationship with his girlfriend. He had gone through so much drama with her that he finally had her removed from his house, but we were still not on speaking terms. I heard that she had been stealing from him and he found out. I never did ask, but was relieved to hear that she was gone. I was learning this information from others. My dad tried to make several attempts to be nice and talk to me, but I was angry about the past, and had not gotten over all the things that we went through that I believed he didn't do anything to make it right. He had a new woman, but she was different. I didn't know then, but I learned later that she was a Christian. She was praying for my dad and encouraging him to make sure he had a relationship with his children and grandchildren. I wasn't ready for a relationship with him yet because I felt like I was making it on my own without him, and that he wasn't there for me when I needed him so there was no need to be daddy now that I was grown. My brother was now married and had his own family. I had another sister from a relationship my dad had. She was older than my brother and I. She lived with my dad for a very short period while trying to get on her feet, but she had moved in with my dad's sister. I went to see her and as we talked, I heard all the stories over again from my sister as to how this lady treated her. It was the same way she had treated us. That is why she was living with my aunt. She was also hurt and angry, but I had no advice for her because I was still angry myself.

Growing up my aunts and uncles would tell me I was

smart, and this encouraged me to try and do whatever I could to become successful. I just didn't have a clue of what real success was. It started with me trying to find a way out of this horrible mess I felt that I had made out of my life. I was in the most abusive relationship, two kids, and no money. I remember one time I was so desperate to get away from him, I jumped out of the car, and took off running as he was coming close to a stop sign.

Everyone knew he could drive better than the average race car driver. He slung the car around to go in the direction I was going, and snatched it in park, and chased me down. I can't tell you the rest that happened because I have no memory of it. When I came to after I guess he hit me, I looked around and realized I was at his mother's house.

The next day I looked in the mirror with black eyes. As I looked at myself in the mirror, I began to have feelings of just being tired of life, but I shook it off because I knew I had to figure it out and keep going. I felt that I had to do something, and do it quickly. I knew all the connections that my children's father had in order to get large quantities of drugs from. They were all attracted to me because they often tried flirting with me when he wasn't around. They were Haitian men that would go back and forth to Haiti and from here to Florida at different times. You would never see them all at once. I began to communicate with them. I wanted to show them that I could make money, and not blow my chance because I was a young female. I didn't know all the ins and outs about it but it didn't take me long to learn. I needed to support my kids and me and get out of the relationship. I had gained all of their trust. They began to bring me Kilos of cocaine, and I was starting to make money. I got my own place. I was really taking a stand letting him know that I no longer wanted a relationship with him, and if I needed to, I would call the police. I did everything possible for him not to know where I lived.

One night a few of my friends and I were at my place. We knew the door was locked, but in the middle of the night we woke up to him standing right over us. He told us all he wanted was for me to get up and talk to him. I did so that it wouldn't be any problems for us. I got in the car with him and he began telling me again all the ways he would change and to just give him another chance. I didn't want to say anything to make him mad so I just put it off on the kids that I needed to get back so I could get them from my aunt and I told him we could talk about it later. I kept reminding him of the kids because I was really in fear that this may be the end of my life.

My friends went down to my brother's house and told him because they thought this was probably the last time they would see me. Everyone was relieved when I got back but I wondered how he knew where I lived and how he had gotten into the house. I left that place soon after that because now I was making money to live anywhere I wanted. I could make one trip and make $15,000 - $19,000 easy. Some time had passed and the guy that cared a lot about me when I was in Massachusetts missed me and wanted to start a new life with me in North Carolina. When he moved in the children's father found out. He began calling my phone twenty-four seven and telling me this was the reason that I didn't want to be back with him because I had brought my new friend down to live with me. One day he and some guy came to my house with a shotgun wrapped in a sheet. He snatched the front storm door open, and unwrapped the gun from under the sheet. When I saw the gun, I pushed the gun down towards the floor causing him to shoot himself in the leg. I began to scream, telling my friend to run out the back door. As he was running out the back door towards my brother's house, the kids' father pointed the gun and shot it. I thought for sure my friend had gotten away. As the kids' father and the guy got in the car and drove quickly away, I went to look for my friend and saw him on the ground down the street. I ran towards him panicking! When I got there he was in pain holding his arm. I called the ambulance and police telling them everything that happened. They got him to the hospital, and luckily he was hit only in the arm. The children's father also needed medical attention because he shot himself in the leg because I pushed the gun down. The police arrested him in the hospital and located the guy driving the get away car and arrested him too. My sons' father was convicted and sentenced to five years for shooting my friend, and this is what finally ended that horrible relationship.

I had been talking to a friend of my children's father. We also knew each other from school. He seemed very nice to my children and I; it was evident hat he had a desire to help take care of us. He was also known to sell drugs so I began to front him drugs and allow him to bring the money back to me. I began to spend time with him, and one thing led to another. We got married. Unfortunately, it was not a good marriage. Looking back, it seemed like he was mainly my protector, and never wanted me to suffer any harm. He would just make sure I was ok. He had no children and he took care of mine as though they were his own. He was a great father to the boys, and he loved them. He was sleeping around before we were married and it didn't stop. It was a constant struggle getting calls or finding a hidden cell phone, which is how I learned of his infidelity. I was simply just fed up with it all, and began to do the same thing he was doing.

I began having an affair with one of my business associates in the drug trade name Ryan. I knew it was wrong, and two wrongs didn't make a right, but Ryan showed love to my children and me. He purchased me a ring and everything. He would go out and buy my boys clothes just because he had them on his mind. He would buy us anything and do anything for us. He wanted to always take me out of town on trips. He desired for me to leave my husband, and move in with him. He had a huge home as well and his own business, and if I wanted to stop selling the drugs he definitely could take care of us. He really wanted me to stop, but I was too far in. I never wanted to be in a position to have to depend on a man ever again after getting out of the relationship with my children father. I wanted my own money and for no man to be able to try and control me on any level because I would have my own. My husband had learned of the affair, but never said a word about knowing until one day I had purchased a brand-new Mercedes Benz, and someone had told him that Ryan purchased it for me, but he didn't. When I pulled up in the driveway with the new car he came out in the yard, and snatched me out of the car, and began to kick the doors in, burst the windows and flatten all the tires. I ran, and called the police and Ryan to tell him what was going on. The police came but my husband had left. I called my aunt and uncle to come to the house because I was terrified that my husband would come back and want to fight. My aunt and uncle came, I left with them, and Ryan was right there to pick me up from my aunt house. He wanted to make sure I was okay, and for me to stay at his house that night or as long as I wanted. However, the next day I left because I had to pick up my kids. Ryan made sure that he took care of everything with the car getting repaired and sold it. He made sure that since the rumor was that he purchased the first car that I had, he would really help me get the second one. We went and ordered another Mercedes and paid $137,000 for the car. I'd already had other luxury cars and trucks. Ryan knew my husband was cheating on me because he would see him at the club with women. Ryan didn't understand why I would be at home and my husband was always out in the street. Ryan was like me; he would rather be at home spending time with a person of interest than out at the club.

By the time I reached the age of 23. We were making so much money! I know that we had wasted over a half million dollars by this time. I recall having over $150,000 dollars in my closet just because, and spending, thousands weekly on just whatever. I had the luxuries of the world and everything money could buy, but for some reason I was not happy on the inside. I constantly felt unhappy. *For what will it profit a man if he gains the whole world, and loses his own soul? (Mark 8:36*

NKJV). I opened two businesses and had become very wealthy with those streams of income and drug money. I had several bank accounts and they all had thousands of dollars in each account. I had money everywhere. Years had passed. The plan was to stop selling drugs, and to just run my businesses, but I am sure that is always the plan with everyone involved that finally get caught. In April, my husband at the time had to go to court for a traffic ticket. I heard my phone ring around 9:30 that morning. He was calling to tell me that the Feds were waiting on him in the courtroom he was directed. He immediately let me know that he was gone because he had been in trouble a few times, but only local state charges. He told me which parking deck the vehicle was parked in when he drove to court and to make sure that I came to get it. I immediately searched to try and get him the best attorney that money could buy. As people began to find out that the Feds had him and that I was searching for an attorney, a guy I'd known for quite some time began to tell me about seeking protection and how he knew people in South Carolina that could do things to make certain situations go away. I was desperate to try and get help to get him out of jail. We had never heard anything good about the Feds. I also wanted to make sure I didn't get locked up as well because I had two sons ten and eleven years old, and I was the only parent they had. I took the drive to South Carolina with my friend and met the people he was talking about. They told me just like he did that they could make it go away and that they would make sure I was protected so that I wouldn't get caught up with the Feds. I took a few more trips down there for the next three weeks that price ranged from 2,000 to 10,000 dollars.

I had entered the world of witchcraft and doing what these people were telling me to do. They would do their chanting and tell me to drink something they had made up, and do all their rituals. I constantly felt uneasy, and at the point of frustration. I had seen a lot of people participate in witchcraft, and knew that this was not really something that I totally agreed with, but I was desperate. I soon learned after a lot of wasted money that these people were just money gimmicks and had no real source of power from God or anything else! All they had that I could sense was some sort of evilness about them. The enemy has a counterfeit for everything that God has created, and this was nothing of God. I was spending money everywhere trying to find him a way out.

One particular night I looked around in the large home that the drug money acquired, and I began to ask myself what was the point of having it all when I had no peace, and I was tired. At that moment my eyes glued in on a bible that I had purchased a year prior, I dusted it off, and turned to Psalm 23. I had always heard people speak about Psalm 23. At the same time my two sons were coming into my bedroom. They both asked, "Momma what's wrong?" I had the bible out on the bed in my hand turned to Psalms 23. I kneeled down on my knees and quoted Psalm 23 twice. At that moment I grabbed my oldest son in one arm and the youngest son in the other arm. I began to cry with tears streaming down my face to God, "Lord I am tired, I know that if there is a God there has to be a better plan for my life than this." My mind was still racing as to try to fix things myself through money and people I knew.

The next day, an associate called me asking me if I could get him a Kilo of cocaine. His girlfriend and I had attended college together and that is how I met him. She had introduced us because she saw all the glamorous cars

I would drive and the nice clothes and jewelry. With making all the money, I was paying my way through school. I actually held on to the words of my aunts and uncles, telling me how smart I was as a young child. It made the impression with me that education and learning were good things. I considered her and I good friends, but looking back, I wonder if she knew her boyfriend as well as she thought she did. He had got into some trouble with the Federal government for selling drugs and this wasn't his first rodeo. He was hip to the federal system and had learned the ropes as to how to stay free or to make it where he would get a short sentence. I didn't know this guy was in his mid- forties until everything unfolded and I began to learn the truth about him. We were all in our twenties and he had me fooled. I knew within, something wasn't right with the call, but I had known him and her for years so I thought to myself maybe I am just paranoid due to everything that was happening. We agreed to meet at a certain place at a certain time. I had an older cousin who would normally go with me to do drug runs because he had an addiction, and he would get drugs from me rather than having to buy them. The drugs would be his payment. As we were going to this place to meet, I began to see cars that didn't look right. The windows were tinted so dark that you couldn't see who were in the vehicles. I began to panic, and called the guy, and asked him what was going on. He knew I was on to him so I proceeded to turn around and go back to where my youngest son was because my oldest son was in the back seat of the car and all I could think about was something is not right and he is with me. The Feds knew that I knew what was going on and they began to follow me. I went to pull into where my youngest son was and the Federal Officers surrounded us from every direction. My baby boy came running out the door. He was running towards me and I looked at him seeing tears running down his face. He was always a true mama's boy. I told him to go back in the house. I told him I would be back as I was handcuffed and put in the back of the police car.

While on the drive downtown to the federal building in the back seat of the car with multiple thoughts racing in my mind, I believed that I would make bail and be out soon. The federal government now wanted to learn more from me. I didn't know they had already interrogated my cousin and he told them everything that he possibly could think of to say and added some things that they may have wanted to hear. The detectives thought that I would be like my cousin and just say whatever, but I was being cautious. Growing up we always believed that officers didn't mind locking us up and throwing away the key, and I truly didn't know much about the federal system. They wanted to know whatever information I knew, and when I asked for an attorney they wanted to make it hard on me because they wanted to build more cases against others. They believed I was their key. Ryan had tried to get the best lawyer for me that he could find. He didn't care how much it cost. We didn't trust any lawyers in the state of North Carolina. We felt they all worked together in this system. He hired me an attorney from Miami, Florida that was said to be the best that had handled many federal drug charges and had great success. I went before the judge. They told me no bail and sent me to a twenty-three hour lock down facility with only one hour out per day to shower and make a ten-minute phone call. The judge said I was a flight risk due to the amount of money they believed I could get my hands on. My attorney appealed, and I went before a judge two days later, and got the same results. I was denied and sent back to the twenty-three hour holding facility. I laid there on my bunk looking up at the ceiling just thinking back over my life, three days before I had every materialistic thing that I wanted, a nice home, cars, clothes, money, jewelry you name it, now I was in a cell without a window to even look out of, and being told I may end up with life in prison for conspiracy to sell drugs, a possibility to be in prison for the rest of my life. I had heard of double jeopardy before, but I thought it was a new term for what I was going through (triple Jeopardy). I have never heard of that term, and it probably does not exist, but that is what I felt. The Feds had wanted the proceeds from the sale of the house; they had taken all the electronic items in my home, and seized all the cars. The state of North Carolina had charged me a penalty to pay taxes on the drugs, had taken all of the four wheelers, jewelry, furniture, lawn mowers, and any other household items that the Feds didn't take, and the feds were also trying to send me to prison for thirty years to life. It seemed like I had every form of government, state and federal officers wanting something from me. The most hurtful part was that once the government got what they wanted, my husband's family went into the house to see what was left so they could take it. It wasn't all of them, but a few. I thought they would be trying to help us but they were trying to see what was still in the house that they could help themselves to. I didn't know what to think or do. I was lost without words and just silent in thought, and every time I called home it was more depressing. My kids would always ask when I was coming home, or my mom would tell me how the detectives were still searching for someone else that could have been involved with me having that lifestyle. As I have always said, my brother and I had always been close. He took my sons in his home. He already had three children; my brother and I both knew that his wife didn't want them there. My brother kept them anyway. I remember calling one time and his wife was telling me how she was going to let social services get my children. I guess the stress of having so many children was taking a toll on her. I finally got to talk to my brother, crying, and he told me not to worry, they weren't going anywhere. My other family members had their own lives with children and were not able or willing to take in two more kids. I thank my brother, my dad and his new wife for allowing my sons to live in their home. My aunt and uncle let them stay on weekends and brought them to visit or did things for them in school, for that I am forever grateful. Ryan was also there for my children, and did whatever he could to help them and me.

As I lay in that cell for some reason, for the first time that I could remember, I felt at peace in the midst of everything that was going on. It seemed all the burdens from the stress of what I was doing, were lifted. I then immediately realized I had prayed three days before, kneeling down with my children, letting God know that I was tired and to help me. Chills ran over my body just thinking of it. I had always heard *be careful what you ask for*; I didn't see this as help, but I felt peace, although now, I had a ton of other questions. If there is a God how could he take me away from my children? They now had no parent out there. At that moment an outreach minister's voice was heard in the lock down dorm. I asked her from my little food tray hole, "Can you please come here?" She came over to me, and I asked her, "do you know the words to Psalm 23".

She said, "yes."

I asked, "Can you say the words to me?" And because I had no paper I wrote the words in pencil on the floor of the cell. I cited the scripture to myself all night until I memorized it. I have no idea why, but I felt I had to learn this psalm and memorize it.

They finally moved me to another county jail where I could be out of my cell. One Sunday morning, I woke up to ministers coming in the jail. They were singing, and wow could they sing. I went over to where they were, and they were telling us about the love of God, and his Son, Jesus Christ who died for all of us and no matter what we thought we did wrong, He would forgive us if we asked. In this jail we could have bibles and I began to read, and cry because here I was twenty-seven years old and was being told that I wouldn't ever be out to be with my kids again. I hated to call home because they would continue to ask, "Ma when are you coming home?" I couldn't dare tell them what I was told. I often thought about Karen at this time. I had never heard from her since we were in Black Mountain together as pregnant teenagers. I was wondering how her life had turned out looking at my own, and I had always desired to see her again.

My attorney would fly from Florida to come visit me and things just were not looking good at all. Every time he had to come from Florida to visit me he charged an enormous amount of money. This time he came he brought me all of my indictment charges for me to read, and when I looked at the papers it said UNITED STATES OF AMERICA vs. TRESSA DELILAH BRANTLEY. I looked at the paper saying to myself "what is this?" The United States of America; who am I to go up against the United States. Out of all the years of hearing "the Feds", I never put two and two together that they were one in the same. I'd never thought of it that way. I sat there and pondered who can win this? The Feds wanted to know everything. They had been told that I was taking over the drug running since my husband was locked up, and that I had did this on another occasion when he did time in state prison for some other charges. I learned this from reading his indictment papers. The authorities were getting their information from statements made by people who were ready to testify against him.

I was scared because what they had heard from the streets was totally wrong. They believed it was my husband that had this entire life style set up because he had been in and out of jail for drugs from a teenager. They already had him in custody and wanted to build this strong case against him. They wanted me to be a witness for them, and they would cut me a deal from this time that they were threatening me with. They told me about the mandatory minimum for drug charges. They were already saying I was going to get thirty years to life. There was no way I could tell these people anything. I would be telling them more information, but it would be on myself not on my husband as they thought. They believed that since my husband was incarcerated that I was taking over from where he left off. As I learned more from my attorney on how all this led up to this, the Feds will tell you they've been watching you for so many years, but the truth is, they find people that know you or folks who are already in custody who will talk. They find out how long they have known you in that lifestyle, and this is how they say they were watching you for several years, and so on.

Most times it is the witness that they have to testify on you or several witnesses that know you that are trying to get out of their trouble. My attorney from Florida told me he wanted to give me some advice. He said that he had already talked to the prosecutor and he could get me a good deal and I could be out in possibly two years. All I needed to do was talk to them so that I can see my children again. He even told me if I talked with them and if they brought pictures in and the detectives point to someone specific to say that I knew them. I told my attorney I wasn't doing that, and he said I am just trying to help you. He said people do it all the time. This is how it works my attorney told me. I told him I was just going to trust and believe God. My attorney got up, banged the wall yelling, "I have been dealing with the feds for over twenty years and God hasn't opened up the flood gates of Heaven for them so don't think that he is going to open them up for you when you get your thirty years." I began to cry not knowing what to think, because I was saying something I had heard others say, to trust God, but I really didn't know God. I asked him "you don't believe in God." He told me "No, I don't believe in none of that crap." Growing up I would always hear people say *trust in God* anytime a bad situation came up. I called my aunt who I knew went to church, and told her what the attorney told me. I just knew she would have some advice for me. She said that she would give my attorney a call, and to give her a call back. When I called her back. She said that he told her the same thing that he told me, and she didn't know what to tell me to do. This was one of my aunts who attended church often, and would encourage me to go. I had high hopes that when I called her back she was going to be able to tell me something good about my statement that I had made to this attorney that I was going to believe and trust God. When she told me she didn't know what to tell me to do. I felt lost, confused, and frustrated because I wanted to follow this God that she had been encouraging me to follow, and go to church to learn about when I was home, but now after he told her what he told me she really didn't know what to tell me. That really silenced me! I was just clueless as what to do. My aunt meant no harm, she just didn't know what to tell me or have any answers for me. She had never known a situation like this, but she answered every time I called, and attended every court date. I guess at the time I was just looking for words of comfort. *But seek first the kingdom of God and His righteousness, and all these things shall be added to you." (Matthew 6:33 NKJV)*

I hung the phone up and went back to my cell. I just cried and looked over at the bible. I began to ask God if He was real, He had to help me and show me that He was real. I began to read my bible. I had spent a ton of money on an attorney that was advising me to do wrong, by cooperating with officers to say I knew people even if I didn't know them when I was already in a bad situation. I couldn't believe this was real or even happening. I felt that he was getting paid all this money to tell me that he really couldn't do anything for me, except tell me to talk to the detectives and lie on someone else if I had to in order to build another case for them. This was the same thing the detectives had been telling me to do all along, for free. I told Ryan, and told him to find me another attorney because this one was charging all this money to tell me what the detectives has been telling me to do. I really felt I do not have a defense attorney. He searched and called many attorneys, and as he explained my case to them, they all began to tell him the same thing. They were willing to take the case, but there was another enormous fee. It was time to go to court again, and I had already signed the papers to withdraw the attorney from Florida, but I never did hire another one. They all had told Ryan that the Florida attorney had given me the best advice to cooperate with the detectives. I agreed to get a Federal Public Defender and not spend any more money. At this time, I had remembered what the singing ministers told me about Jesus Christ and I wanted to accept Him as my Lord and Savior. I remembered them saying, *if you confess with your mouth the Lord Jesus and believe in your heart that God has raised him from the dead, you will be saved. For with the heart one believes unto righteousness, and with the mouth confession is made unto salvation. (Romans 10:9-10 NKJV)* It was something different about these ministers. As I began to study the word, I immediately remembered at a very young age when Brenda was in our life she would let my brother and I catch a church bus that came through where we lived from time to time. On this particular night that we had went. We went to the altar and kneel down to accept the Lord as small children at a revival. I had never in my life had this memory. *Yet the helper, the Holy Spirit, whom the Father will send in My name, He will teach you all things, and bring to your remembrance all things that I said to you. (John 14:26 NKJV)*

I had been learning so much from the bible. I didn't think on me being in jail so much anymore or everything that was going on with my situation. I couldn't believe what I was reading. I began to learn about how the choices you make allow your life to be under the blessing or under a curse, but we now had Jesus that gives us grace so that we all can be blessed. I began to get answers to my questions that I had been asking the Lord. *"The Lord will send on you cursing, confusion, and rebuke, in all that you set your hand to do, until you are destroyed, and until you perish quickly, because of the wickedness of your doings in which you have forsaken me."* *(Deuteronomy 28:20 NKJV)* I had accepted Christ as a child, but I had forsaken him and turned to witchcraft and every other human idol. I didn't understand it then, but I understand it now, as I couldn't remember hearing the name Jesus Christ growing up. I just heard everyone say God, but a pastor told me, that I didn't remember it because I didn't have a spiritual ear to hear. I wanted to know why I had to lose my house that I had built. *"You shall build a house, but you shall not dwell in it."* *(Deuteronomy 28:30 NKJV)* I wanted to know if there was a God why am I not raising my children. *"Your sons and daughters shall be given to another people, and your eyes shall look, and fail with longing for them all day long; and there shall be no strength in your hand."* *(Deuteronomy 28:32 NKJV)* As I read the word with my eyes glued to the pages, all of my questions were being answered. I wondered how could this be. This is my life being told to me from a book that my hands were holding. *That which was from the beginning, which we have heard, which we have seen with our eyes, which we have looked upon, and our hands have handled, concerning the Word of life. (I John 1:1 NKJV)* I was under the curse because I had forsaken God with the choices I made with my life. I found me in the bible, my life being explained to me in a way I had never known. *"My people are destroyed for lack of knowledge, I also will reject you from being priest for me; because you have forgotten the law of your God, I also will forget your children." (Hosea 4:6 NKJV)*

I had been angry for years and mainly with my childhood life. I had tried to build happiness and success with my own hands. The more I read the more I was being healed. I truly wanted to change. I wanted this God that I was saying I would trust in. I realized that I couldn't be mad at my parents. I began to look at my own parenting and how I am now a mother in jail, and can't even touch my kids. I was seeing that my parents did their best with the knowledge they had, and that life didn't come with a parenting manual.

Parenting comes with experience and guidance. They made some bad choices, but I couldn't hold that against them. My parents were human and in need of a Savior just like I was. I began to learn that we can all make many choices in our life, but none of us can choose our parents. God gave them to me, and that was His purpose. I had no choice in the matter of who my mother was and I had no choice in the matter of who my father was. God did the choosing and I needed to love them, and forgive them. So that I could be set free. *"But if you do not forgive, neither will your father in heaven forgive your trespasses." (Matthew 6:14 NKJV)* I realized no one could choose his or her family members, that is all God's doing. *"Before I formed you in the womb I knew you; before you were born I sanctified you;" (Jeremiah 1:5 NKJV)* I had always heard as a child that it takes a village to raise a child. I also didn't know what my parents had gone through raising me. I stopped the blame game and began to start taking some responsibility for where I was in life; how I began to make wrong choices, yet I was changing on the inside. There was no more pointing the fingers. I needed to work on me. *"Therefore, my beloved, as you have always obeyed, not as in my presence only, but now much more in my absence, work out your own salvation with fear and trembling; for it is God who works in you both to will and to do for His good pleasure." (Philippians 2:12-13 NKJV)* Rather than being bitter, I was grateful that I was still alive. Grateful that I still had parents alive. Years of dealing drugs as a woman and never being robbed or hurt; all the negative things that come with that lifestyle, I had only heard about them, never actually experiencing it myself.

Months had gone by and I was submerged in reading all I could about God. I began reading free, spiritual books that were sent from Kenneth Copeland Ministries. This preacher explained the Word of God so simply to me and I learned a lot from him. I began to call him my spiritual father when I'd never met him a day in my life. I learned that he would send books and bibles, and all sorts of learning material absolutely free. All you had to do was send a letter and request it. I did this numerous times and not once was I ever sent a letter back saying I would not be able to get the material. This ministry sent scriptural material every time. I realized I couldn't learn what I hadn't been taught. I had no interest in what everyone else had to say or what they were doing. All I wanted to know was what the bible said. I immersed myself in the word of God and Min. Copeland's teachings, and applied what he taught to my life. I always saw something he would say, but it seemed too good to be true and I would look in the bible for myself. I never found one thing in his books that I couldn't confirm in the scripture. I took the time to make sure because I wanted to know the truth about God; no story telling stuff, anymore.

The county jail I was in became over crowded and some had to sleep on the floor. I was one of them so I was moved to another county jail. It didn't bother me. Once I got to the next jail. I would send Kenneth Copeland Ministry another letter and they would send me material again FREE! I had accepted Jesus Christ as my Savior. I kept saying to myself it couldn't be this easy, there had to be more. I didn't "feel" saved but I was constantly told salvation was by faith. I believed I was saved because I believed God and I believed that the Bible was His word, and if the Word said it, I had to be, as long as I did what the Bible told me to do in order to be saved. I just couldn't fathom that I would give my all to the enemy, but not to God and He is the creator of all things. I knew He loved me and wanted me blessed, but I needed to get my life in line with the blessing. Anytime that you are called to be a witness, even in the natural, its trusted that you have some evidence or proof of what you experienced. I wanted this power and to be a witness that had evidence.

The word confirmed I was saved, but I began to see the scriptures referenced a baptism in the Spirit. I read multiple scriptures that referenced each other. *"For John truly baptized with water, but you shall be baptized with the Holy Spirit not many days from now." (Acts 1:5 NKJV).* This clearly showed me this was something separate from water baptism. Water and Spirit are not the same things. I had seen many practice the water baptism, that Jesus said could be done by man because John was a man, but what about this other baptism that was being promised from the Father. Jesus told them to wait for? It also spoke of receiving power to be an effective witness for Christ once the Holy Spirit comes upon you. I wanted to be his witness for sure on earth. *"But you shall receive power when the Holy Spirit has come upon you; and you shall be witnesses to Me in Jerusalem, and in all Judea and Samaria, and to the end of the earth."*

(Acts 1:8 NKJV). While continuing to study, I had been praying a prayer that I saw in one of Kenneth Copeland's books. I researched these scriptures and the Holy Spirit was showing me about praying for the baptism in the Holy Spirit as the first Church received in the book of Acts. I prayed the prayer time and time again. On this particular day, I was in my cell giving God praise just for being God, and when I prayed this prayer in faith. *"If you then, being evil, know how to give good gifts to your children, how much more will your heavenly Father give the Holy Spirit to those that ask Him!" (Luke 11:13 NKJV)*

I was in the cell alone and it was if I heard wind. This was in the middle of the summer, and my teeth began to shiver as if it was in the brink of winter, but it was hot. I couldn't stop it, and I began to pray in an unknown tongue. *"They were all filled with the Holy Spirit and began to speak with other tongues, as the Spirit gave them utterance". (Acts 2:4 NKJV)*

As I lay back on the bunk it seemed like I was experiencing something roaming over my heart, and the mid-section of my body. *"I will give you a new heart and put a new spirit within you; I will take the heart of stone out of your flesh and give you a heart of flesh. (Ezekiel 36:26 NKJV)* Everything was changing. I swore a lot, but now I hated the sound of a curse word. It was just me; sitting in that cell by myself praising God in my jail uniform with corn rolls. God did all this for me just the way I was, no fancy car, no fancy house, jewelry, money, husband, or anything else that I had lost or that was of the world. It was just God and me! I will praise him all the days of my life. I didn't have to find the right outfit, or shoes to wear, or remove my tattoos so I could receive His free gift. God deals with us on individual basis. He will work with you in the area in which you need him to and He knows what each of us need. I realized that I hardly ever went to church because of religion. You had to dress like this or wear that. Religion would say, 'God don't like this, God don't like that', but there I was sitting in a jail and God was right there with me loving me and fulfilling His word and promises to me. God cared about my soul, not my outward appearance. I began to notice I was having a relationship with God rather than being religious with a ton of legalistic rules of the do's and don'ts. This relationship caused me to want to do right and honor

God in everything I did. I came to God just as I was but he didn't allow me to stay as I was. The Holy Spirit was at work doing His job, the work that only He could do. I would just lie there and talk to God about everything. I would see women coming in and out of jail. I would see them come in addicted to drugs. I would ask God to forgive me for anything that I had done to sale drugs to anyone, since I was dealing on a larger scale. I never saw the horrible everyday affects that it had on the lives of the users and their families. I was deeply grieved in my spirit by what I was seeing. The women would leave jail all cleaned up looking nice and I would see them right back in a month or so and they looked terrible. I heard all kinds of stories from younger woman, sixteen and seventeen, as to their parents selling them for drugs and then they eventually became addicted. I was so heart broken, and wanted every woman in the jail to learn of the hope I was receiving from the Bible.

Soon after, I began to teach bible study and as I taught, I didn't realize that I learned the scriptures so well. They were springing up as living water coming out. *"He who believes in Me, as the Scriptures said, out of his heart will flow rivers of living water" (John 7:38 NKJV).* When I would have bible study the guards in the jail would listen and enjoy. The ministers loved to come into the jail. One minister told me that the peace of God was resting upon me. They also enjoyed seeing the women learning about Christ. The Holy Spirit living in me needed a voice, and I said, "Lord, here I am use mine". I taught them everything I knew even if I had just learned it. A few of them had told me I gave them hope because they had been coming to jail seeing women come in and go out, but I was grasping what they were teaching and they saw it. I was excited to see them as well.

Now just because I was saved didn't mean that things turned around automatically, in fact, trouble would often head my way. There were multiple things always going on in jail. One day a woman twice my size was locked up. This woman was my Goliath. She cursed me out for no reason and would often threaten me, one time threatening to throw me over the banister of the stairwell. As she was walking up the stairs I prayed to God to help me. I couldn't just stand there so I knew I needed to get to the bottom of the stairs before she came up the stairs, because I wasn't going to give her the opportunity to grab me at that height. I started walking towards her as she was trying to make her way up. As I was approaching the staircase a lady in front of me named Donna whom I had befriended sharing bible notes with, took her fist, and knocked the lady out cold. I looked at Donna, and she looked at me and said, "what I was not going to let her get up those stairs to attempt to do anything to you". I just smiled and thank the Lord, because that was one big lady. As I sat there thinking about this incident knowing that I didn't do anything to this lady, I realized that the enemy wanted to silence the voice that was bringing God's word forth. I implore you do not allow the enemy to silence your voice being used by God. I was doing all I could do to walk with God because I had read in His word that I had to agree with Him in order to walk with Him. *"Can two walk together unless they are agreed?" (Amos 3:3 NKJV)* I applied every word that I'd learned in the bible to my life. I carefully reviewed to see if the scriptures were written for past, present, or future tense.

I recall another instance one day after having bible study, I was awake and I saw an image that appeared in front of my face that was identical to mine, but the image had no eyes. Each way I turned my face, the image turned its face the same way, but it had no eyes. I kept looking at it because it was an exact match as to what I looked like and it turned its face the same way I turned mine. I asked the image, "Where are your eyes", it didn't respond. So, you can imagine I was quite confused. That night one of the ministers came to visit us and the moment I heard her I ran to tell her what happened earlier. "Mrs. Brooks", I said, "I do not know what is going on but there was an image that came out of me that looked like my face, but it had no eyes. Each way I turned my face the image turned its face, but it had no eyes." She looked at me and said, "Honey the Lord is doing a major work in you. That image you saw was you. It had no eyes because you had been walking in darkness so long you couldn't see. No person can see without eyes, but the Lord has lifted the veil off your face and has given you spiritual eyes, and now you can see." *"But their minds were blinded for until this day the same veil remains uplifted in the reading of the Old Testament, because the veil is taken away in Christ, but even this day, when Moses is read, a veil lies on their heart. Where the Spirit of the Lord is there is liberty. But we all, with unveiled face beholding as in a mirror the glory of the Lord, are being transformed into the same image from glory to glory, just as by the Spirit of the Lord". (II Corinthians 3:14-18 NKJV)* I cried and praised God, because He chose me and was working on me after all I had done. He removed my spiritual blindness so that I could walk in the light and see spiritual things. I was experiencing the Lord and His word was confirming and witnessing to my heart. The veil had been removed and I was seeing with spiritual eyes. I whole-heartedly turned to the Lord and he knew it.

Anger, rebellion, bitterness, lies, unforgiveness, adultery, fornication and strife will keep you in spiritual darkness, and can paralyze you in your spirit. No one owed me anything. I owed it all to the Lord for helping me. He redeemed my life from destruction. *"Who redeems your life from destruction, who crowns you with lovingkindness and tender mercies." (Psalms 103:4 NKJV)* Every time Evangelists would come into the jail they would tell me God was going to use me mightily. I often wondered how none of these people knew each other and only knew me from in the jail, but they all would say the same thing. *"God is going to use you mightily."* I met another lady while in jail who became my friend. She actually is one of the ones who noticed the prophetic confirmation amongst the ministers. She said to me, "Tressa, how is it that no matter which minister comes in here they always pick you out of the bunch and say the same thing. God is going to use you mightily?" I said, "You know what? I don't know." This was the beginning when I learned about prophecy and how God would confirm His word by two or three witnesses. *"This will be the third time I am coming to you. By the mouth of two or three witnesses every word shall be established" (II Corinthians 13:1 NKJV)*

They all had the same Spirit so they didn't have to know each other or me. They had the same Spirit of Christ. *"There is one body and one Spirit, just as you were called in one hope of your calling" (Ephesians 4:4 NKJV)* I would study day after day. At this time when my attorney, the public federal defender, would come, she would want to talk about my case, but I would be talking about the Lord. One time she told me every time she came to visit me she would leave inspired, and that she had never met anyone like me before. There were still things going on with my case, but I constantly stayed in prayer and in God's word.

In prison and on the streets, it is known to not be a snitch. This word snitch is a term to make people feel horrible about telling the truth. Many people fear being called this word, and it is keeping people in bondage by not telling the truth that will set them free. I recall a day where God showed me a spiritual vision of me being entangled in spider webs. These webs had me bound so tight I could not move or break free. The Lord began to show me that this word "snitch" was part of the enemy of our soul's cunningness and craftiness because he does nothing original. The Lord is the truth and the light. The enemy is darkness and deception. The Lord showed me every time I told a lie, I would entangle myself with another web, but if I told the truth the webs would begin to break. The enemy would not be able to hold me in that darkness anymore or keep me in bondage because telling the truth would expose the lie. *"Put away from you a deceitful mouth, and put perverse lips far from you (Proverbs 4:24 NKJV)* As I studied this word, and saw that this is a form of the enemy's devices, all this time I had feared telling the truth, *"…let God be true, but every man a liar…'* (Romans 3:4 NKJV) Although I repented to God, I still had to follow His direction and be faithful to His word, and not my own so that God could help me. God won't go against His own word because He is the Word. *"He who works deceit shall not dwell within my house; he who tells lies shall not continue in my presence" (Psalms 101:7 NKJV)* As the Lord showed me I had to tell the truth even if it was detrimental to me, I realized that a snitch was actually a person who tells the truth about a situation. *"Then you will know the truth and the truth will set you free" (John 8:32)* I spoke with Ryan and told him everything the Lord had been showing me, and he clearly saw the miraculous change in my life. I sent a letter to my husband who was still awaiting sentencing for his conspiracy charges. He would have rather taken the time than snitch on his wife. We had issues throughout our marriage, but when things got tough we always stood in there together without question. We exchanged letters and at one point we were in the same county jail and because we were married, they allowed us to communicate through security glass. I told him all the things that I was learning from the Lord, and that I had decided to talk with detectives. He disagreed. I explained everything to him, how the Lord explained it to me. I had him convinced he had to tell the truth even if it was against me. It was the right thing to do because I was still holding on and trusting God. I made sure that he knew. I was going to talk to the authorities and tell them the whole truth. I was the organizer of everything all the businesses, the drugs, the houses, cars everything. I told him to contact his lawyer to see if he could arrange for him to talk with detectives after they spoke with me. I wanted them to be able to verify what I was telling them through him, and also make it easier for him as if he wasn't selling me out. I called my attorney, and told her that I would talk to the detectives.

I was also going to inform Ryan that the relationship we had in the past was not acceptable or pleasing to God. I only wanted to be his friend not his girlfriend. I wanted him to find a good person for him that would become his wife. I now saw him as my brother in Christ. I spoke to him about the Lord being his savior and he wanted the Lord. I didn't want anything except what was best for his soul. He wasn't seeing what I was seeing as far as the relationship, but I was more spiritually mature, so I had to be the one to live by the word and do what was right in the sight of God for both of our relationships with Christ. An adulterous relationship was not of God and I refused to take advantage of him. I truly wanted to lead him to Christ so that his soul would be saved. When you know, you are more mature in Christ than your brother or sister you are obligated to walk in Christ so that they may see your true love for them at the right time. That's the most important thing in this life. I didn't want to disappoint God and the love I had found in Christ. My mind had changed in so many areas from studying the word. *"And do not be conformed to this world, but be transformed by the renewing of your mind, that you may prove what is that good and acceptable and perfect will of God." (Romans 12:2 NKJV)* God was at work! I called Ryan the next day. He said he didn't want me to have to say anything about him; he would get an attorney, and go and turn himself in. Ryan asked for me to get the detectives' name and number from my attorney. I got the information and gave it to him, and he set up an appointment to go speak with them. They lied to him. They told him they would meet with him, but before the meeting they tried to find everything they could on him to make sure that they could hold him, making it so that he would not be able to get out on bond. They tried to find every material thing they could to seize from him, the same way they did me. I say this to let everyone know that whatever things you acquire the wrong way, remember, they are only for a season and you will lose it all.

I had been in the county jail over a year. My attorney had arranged for them to come, and so did my husband's attorney. The detectives came and I began to tell them the truth, that I was the one behind the entire operation, not my husband. I was the one who would front him drugs to sale and he would bring the money back along with many others, and how this had started before we were married. They still believed I was covering for my husband, but their instincts told them I knew too much information to simply be a cover up. I told them incriminating information on the transactions that took place, how, when, and where, and with whom. After they interviewed my husband, they realized I was telling the truth, because he had limited information and he couldn't confirm all the questions that they asked. I told them how I had met the guy that set me up and that confirmed his story. After the meeting, I was escorted back to my cell. I felt relieved because it was hard keeping up with a lie. I was nervous because I didn't know where this was going to lead. They continued to tell me that I was facing thirty years to life, but I was still trusting God.

Looking in from the outside it seemed as though I was an absolute idiot but I knew this was the first time in my life that I had made the right decision. I knew that my heart was focused on the Lord and I needed to continue this new process by Truth. *"Examine yourselves as to whether you are in the faith. Test yourselves. Do you not know yourselves, that Jesus Christ is in you?—unless indeed you are disqualified."(II Corinthians 13:5 NKJV)* I knew that I had Jesus Christ. I felt confident in myself, and He was teaching me to love myself, because He loved me. I continued studying God's word, reading praying and meditating. I continued the bible studies and I had found another nugget in the bible. I began to learn about fasting and how God delivered his people as they fasted. I knew the scripture that said God did not show any favorites, and if He did it for them, He would do it for me. *"For God does not show favoritism" (Romans 2:11 NIV)*

Through all of this I understand the first thing God was trying to get me to realize was His love for me. If people do not think that God loves them, they won't believe that He will help them. I began to fast half a day with no food only water. I would go an entire day with nothing but water and just read the word and pray. One day the light bulb came on as I was studying. I came to the scripture. *"Jesus cried out with a loud voice, saying, "Eli, Eli, lama sabachathani?" that is "My God, My God, why have you forsaken Me?" (Matthew 27:46 NKJV)* My eyes were glued to the pages because all I could remember was darkness and not having a relationship with God. I was filled with sorrow just imagining how Jesus felt, I then heard in my spirit those words that had been spoken by Jesus, "My God, My God, why have you forsaken me?" The Lord gave me revelation that Jesus said those words so that I would never have to say them. Immediately the scripture to confirm this came in my mind. *"Let your conduct be without covetousness; be content with such things as you have. For he himself said "I will never leave you nor forsaken you." (Hebrews 13:5 NKJV)* Oh how I felt the love of God at that moment and I truly believed it. All of a sudden it was as if I was in a vision and I could hear. I can't really explain it but I can tell you it seemed as if I was there when Jesus was on the cross. I could hear all the commotion, and as soon as I looked up and saw the cross that Jesus was on, it was if God picked me up and placed me inside the body of Jesus Christ while he was on the cross. It was the realization of the scripture, *"Or do you not know that as many of us as were baptized into Jesus Christ were baptized into his death? Therefore, we were buried with him through baptism into death, that just as Christ was raised from the dead by the glory of the father even so we also should walk in newness of life. For if we have been united together in likeness of his death certainly we also shall be in the likeness of his resurrection, knowing this that our old man __was crucified with him__, that the body of sin might be done away with, that we should no longer be slaves to sin." (Romans 6:3-6 NKJV)* I saw that the word said we were crucified with him. God knew us and knew all of our sins, but His love for us put us there so that Jesus could take all of our sin upon Himself. I then understood what the apostle Paul meant when he said, *"For I through the law died to the*

law that I might live to God. ***I have been crucified with Christ****;
it is no longer I who live, but Christ lives in me; and the life
which I now live in the flesh I live by faith in the Son of God,
who loved me and gave himself for me."(Galatians 2:19-20)*

I really don't have words to express what I felt at that
moment. The experience I had was being revealed to
me IN THE WORD. I learned that in the scriptures
anywhere it said, ***In whom,*** ***In Christ*** *or* ***In him,*** these
words were written so we could learn our true identity in
Christ. *"But God, who is rich in mercy, because of his great love
with which He loved us, even when we were dead in trespasses,
made us alive together with Christ (by grace you have been
saved), and raised us up together, and made us sit together in the
heavenly places in Christ Jesus." (Ephesians 4:2-6 NKJV)*

I hope that as you are reading this book you noticed
the tense that this scripture was written, this is past tense. I
must say God did it all for you and I. We cannot have
Faith except in what was finished. *"Looking unto Jesus the
author and finisher of our faith, who for the joy that was set
before him endured the cross, despising the shame and has sat
down at the right hand of the throne of God." (Hebrews 12:2
NKJV)* He did it all on the cross. God put us there. I
didn't write the book. I just believed every word He said. I

didn't add to it or take anything away. *"Making the word of God of no effect through your tradition which you have handed down. And many such things you do." (Mark 7:13 NKJV)*

I continued to read it just as it was written. In the scriptures, it is revealed that we were raised up together with Christ. We are to live this knew life by faith in His love for us. Jesus died for us and made us new in Him so why would we settle for less? He loved us enough to give His life. God doesn't need any help clarifying what His word says. Sometimes we just need help with believing what He said. *"In the beginning was the word, and the word was with God and the word was God. He was in the beginning." (John 1:1 NKJV)*

A few months had passed and the judge was ready to hand down my sentence. The authorities had already sentenced my husband and things were not good for him. They gave him thirty years in federal prison. I was pleading guilty to my charges, but I still had faith and trusted in God. I prayed to the Lord multiple times for my husband. I believed whatever God did for me that he would also do for him. I thought that he had gotten the bad end of the stick, even though we had told the truth. I had strong Faith. No one could tell me anything different about God. I no longer saw the judge as my judge, I saw God as my judge. I didn't see my attorney as the attorney as when I first met her, I saw her as the vessel God had chosen to work through for my case.

I was waiting in the back holding cell waiting for them to call my name. I was sitting there, the only female being sentenced that day. My attorney told me the prosecutor was recommending that I get a sentence of sixteen years and five-years federal probation. That was not what I wanted to hear. It was better than where I started, but still not what I wanted to hear. I was still trusting in God. Many people went before me and they were all coming back with a lot of time. I still remember saying to myself, I believe the Love that God has for me, and He will deliver and honor me. Now it was my turn to go before the judge. I walked in with these awful looking handcuffs and shackles.

As I walked in I maintained my confidence by thinking of the Lord's goodness, which I knew to be true. I stood before the judge, and the prosecutor spoke his thoughts and gave his sixteen-year prison sentence recommendation for the crimes I had committed. My attorney spoke on my behalf. After she spoke letting the judge know that I was pleading guilty to the charges against me, the judge said he wanted to take a short recess to read over some information.

The judge returned and sentenced me to one hundred and thirty-two months in federal prison. That was eleven years! I looked back at my aunt who was in the courtroom and she began to cry. Tears welled up in my eyes because I was hurting for her having to be there and witness my sentencing. They took me to the back and put me in the holding cell. As I sat down and put my head down in my hands, I began to calculate the years and how old my children would be before I would get out of prison. It would be eleven years before they would have their mother back in their lives. Looking down at the floor a federal guard came to my cell, and asked, "Mrs. Brantley how did you turn out?" Before I could answer the question, I heard in my spirit, "It's not over yet." I looked at the officer and said it went good and I smiled. My lawyer came back to the holding cell to speak with me to ask me if I was ok. She assured me that something happened in there that she has never seen happen before. She said she has never seen this judge take a recess to read over anything before sentencing once the prosecutor gave his recommendation. The prosecutor recommended that I get sixteen years, and the judge came back and gave me eleven years. I knew then that I had to maintain my faith even though I didn't understand since I had just been sentenced to eleven years and five years probation.

They transported me back to the county jail until I could be sent to prison. I went back in the county jail still standing on what I believed from God. I was still teaching bible study and reading His word. I received mail from many of the ladies that I had bible study with in the past. They were grateful and thankful to God and knew God loved them. I would try and write back as many as I could, but I kept being moved, and couldn't keep up with all the letters. I was honored to be able to help someone through the love of God. I was finally sent to Oklahoma. I taught bible study there as well while waiting to get to Alderson Federal Prison in West Virginia. I had finally reached Alderson Federal Prison and to my surprise when I got there all I could see was news reporters, cameras, and a helicopter flying over the camp. I had been studying the Bible so much I didn't watch the news, so I didn't know what was going on. To my surprise the woman across the hall from my room was Martha Stewart. I saw all the others trying to become close to her and befriend her. In the past I would have tried to get under her wings to learn from her but nothing interested me now except God. Jesus was the most famous person that I wanted to know. I wanted the things of the Spirit. We would all be in a certain dorm area until they assigned our main living arrangements while we were in prison. They had assigned my dorm and I had to walk up the hill. When I got up there, I was putting my stuff in my room and as I walked out, I bumped into a young lady. "She said don't I know you?" Immediately when I heard her voice I said, "Karen"? She said, "Tressa?" We hugged! We couldn't believe it. Yes, this was the Karen I met in the Black Mountain Detention center when we were pregnant teenagers. I had always wanted to see her again and I remembered in the County jail I had talked about her to God. Praying for her and hoping that she was all right. I wanted to see her again and God answered my prayer. Karen had been through a lot since we were teenagers. She now had five children. We talked to try and catch up on life. During our conversation, she told me she had been in an altercation and was shot in the back. The bullet couldn't be removed. She would have horrible seizures that would leave her bed ridden at times. She was in federal prison for conspiracy to sell drugs, but Karen also loved the Lord and thanked him for her life.

I met two other ladies that stood out in my life from the time I was in the county jail and now we were in federal prison together. They were a mother and a daughter. Carla was the mother who became like a mother to me, and her daughter became like my sister. We really looked out for one another and loved each other. I constantly confessed my faith to them, and they never criticized me or thought I was crazy like some of the others did. I would share with them many things that I was learning from God. They knew I'd devoted my life to studying the word.

In prison we were assigned jobs at the prison and I was determined to know God by His word. I began to seek God with all my heart, soul and mind. I started fasting. I fasted fourteen days with no food just water. I wanted to be a living sacrifice to God by giving up eating, which I loved to do. *"I beseech you therefore brethren, by the mercies of God, that you present your bodies a living sacrifice, holy, acceptable to God which is your reasonable service." (Romans 12:1 NKJV)* I believed that God would move on my behalf. One day I asked the Lord to help me and I told him He had to teach me more about faith and prayer. I left and went to the dining hall to eat. When I came back there were three books on my desk about faith, prayer, and gifts of the Spirit written by Kenneth Hagan. I had never heard of this minister before. I would always study Kenneth Copeland, and I had read some books by Joyce Meyer. I was shocked that God had answered my request so quickly with those books just showing up on my desk. As I was pondering the miracle, a girl name Arlene walked in my room. She worked the trash crew and she said, "Tressa I saw these brand new spiritual books on the back porch of one of the cottages and as soon as I saw them I knew I needed to give them to you. Can you believe that someone was throwing away brand new books?" I still have these books.

Kenneth Hagan was an awesome man of God and the more I read his books, the more I learned. I was watching Kenneth Copeland on television one day and to my surprise him and his wife were explaining how they learned so much from brother Kenneth Hagan over the years. Now I just knew nothing in my life was coincidental anymore. God was in full control. I knew then God was real and this is not prison for me, it was Bible College! I had full tuition paid in full by the federal government and I just needed to master this class of walking with God. The Lord was even paying for the books and having them delivered to me. I really believed without a doubt I was God's daughter and He was teaching me and training me. I studied those books, and while reading one scripture, Mark 11:23, the Lord spoke to me and said, "A man sees what he says." He repeated it to me three times. So I just said, "Lord why did you say it three times when I heard you the first time." I looked down at the scripture again and realized that it said _say_ three times; it was showing me to keep saying what I believed. *For assuredly, I say to you, whoever __says__ to this mountain, 'Be removed and be cast into the sea,' and does not doubt in his heart, but believes that those things he __says__ will be done, he will have whatever he __says__," (Mark 11:23 NKJV)*

The Lord was showing me I had to speak what I believed, for it to come to pass in my life. I realized everything that I had received from God at that point in my life was because I believed and confessed. I had confessed for God's help, I confessed for salvation, I had confessed for the Baptism in the Spirit. I received all of this by saying His word and speaking it back to him. I had learned many scriptures by that time. I had to speak the word, to write it on my heart so I could believe it and God would bring it to pass. *"My heart is overflowing with a good theme; I recite my composition concerning the King; My tongue is the pen of a ready writer." (Psalms 45:1 NKJV)* I began to confess every day. I was putting God at his word based on the scripture Mark 11:23.

*"I have faith in God. I have the God kind of faith. I say unto this **eleven-year prison sentence** thou shall be removed and be cast into the sea and I do not doubt in my heart but I believe what I say and whatsoever I say I shall have."* I continued praying and fasting. It took me to another level in God. I was hearing clear from God. He had told me He was going to deliver me and honor me. I was still teaching bible studying and sharing what I was learning. The ladies

knew every night at seven o'clock was our bible time and they would be waiting, the young and older ladies. We had an awesome time each night just sharing the word of God.

I was still in communication with my attorney, believing that she would be able to tell me good news one day. She had been working hard trying to help me all she could. She never really wrote any letters, so I was surprised to receive a letter from her. Her letter stated she didn't see anything changing with my sentencing; there was nothing else that could be done. As I read the letter, I would not confess what it said, my friends who were with me, read the letter and consoled me after they read it. Some folks thought I was crazy, and others just said that I had high hopes and they didn't want to disappoint me. There were a lot of women in prison who had already did the time that I was sentenced and still had five or ten more years left, if not more. I still confessed I trusted God. Again, I never confessed from my mouth what the letter said because the Lord had already been dealing with me about, "a man see what he says", and that was not what I wanted to see. I wanted to see my children at home. I put the letter up and also put it away in my mind. I had to obey every step the Lord had given me because I knew disobedience in one step was going to lead to God's silence for the next. I knew this because I found myself repeating steps until I had received them rooted in my heart.

Just when I thought things couldn't get worst, I called home and my mother answered the phone crying, angry fussing at me. She said that my sons' father, who they never liked, had gone to the Sheriff's department and he wanted them from her house without question. The sheriff took him and removed the kids from my mom's house. I called for days with no answer, and finally one day the kids answered, and told me he would unplug the phone unless he was there. My kids said that they had a phone, and told me they would hide it and plug it up at 3:00 when they got home from school so that they could talk to me. They did this for a while until he found out. For some reason my kids' father would always talk to my dad because he respected him. So my dad would come by and check on the boys and keep them on the weekends.

They only gave us 300 minutes a month for phone privileges, and I was trying to check on the kids so much my friends would let me use some of their minutes, and that was against the prison rules. We had all got caught, and we all lost good days for this and our phone privileges for six months. So please do not think that you want make mistakes even when you are doing all you can do to follow the Lord, because out of desperation. I had violated rules and got into trouble. I was back to my only resort, trusting God, and not my own works. I had no way to communicate to my children. I knew of the book of Ester in the bible when God delivered millions of Jews. When they fasted for 3 days. I went to God and I put him at his word. I reminded him that He was no respecter of person. I started my fast, with no food only water, Friday at 9:00 am to Monday at 9:00 am. I declared to God it was finished, because I knew I couldn't have faith in anything except what Jesus had already finished for me on the cross. At 9:00 on the dot it rained so hard. I'd never seen rain like this before in my life. It lasted maybe 2 minutes and then the sun came out. My dad came to see me. He told me he had a surprise for me. He said that the kids' father had come by that Thursday and told him he was giving him the kids because he knew they would be in good hands. My dad said the kids' father told him he didn't know why he was doing it but he just felt like that was what he needed to do (praise God I knew why). He signed the kids over to him and went with my dad to transfer their schools. I told my dad I had fasted and prayed, and I told the Lord Thank you

I began to learn about tithing. This is the only scripture in the word that God tells you to prove him in something. *"Ye are cursed with a curse: for ye have robbed me, even this whole nation. Bring ye all the tithes into the storehouse, that there may be meat in mine house, and prove me now herewith, saith the LORD of hosts, if I will not open you the windows of heaven, and pour you out a blessing, that there shall not be room enough to receive it."* (Malachi 3:9-10 KJV)

Every new principle I learned from God, I applied it to my life. If someone sent me fifty dollars in I would fill a form out to send five dollars to Kenneth Copeland Ministries because I had been so blessed by this ministry. I knew that all the items the ministry had sent me everywhere I'd been was being paid for by someone it wasn't me or the other men and women that were locked up. Kenneth Copeland had partners and I wanted to be one of those partners. I wanted to be a part of this giving and part of another person gaining knowledge like this ministry had done for me. I wanted this opportunity. I had seen media about the negativity where they called this ministry and others, the prosperity teachers, and tried to make them out to look bad. Yet what really amazed me was all this material was available to everyone, but people chose not to dig into it themselves, to see what was really written? God wants you prosperous in every area of life not just material wealth. He wants you spiritually sound and whole. I was seeking and searching for God to restore me with my children and because of His great love I received so much more. *"Ask, and it will be given to you; seek, and you will find; knock, and it will be opened to you. For everyone who asks receives, and he who seeks finds, and to him who knocks it will be opened. Or what man is there among you who, if his son asks for bread, will give him a stone? Or if he asks for a fish, will he give him a serpent? If you then, being evil, know how to give good gifts to your children, how much more will your Father who is in heaven give good things to those who ask Him"* (Matthew 7-7:11 NKJV). It didn't make sense to me that if we had a God that created the heavens and the earth and sent His only begotten son to redeem us that He would want us broke sick, and without His power. The scripture said that His will be done on earth as in heaven, in heaven, He speaks of all good things - joy, peace, happiness, no sickness, no lack. *"In this manner, therefore, pray: Our Father in heaven, Hallowed be Your name. Your kingdom come. Your will be done on earth as it is in heaven. (Matthew 6:9-10 NKJV)* As I continuously read the word the more I read of the blessings of God. *The blessing of the LORD, it maketh rich, and he addeth no sorrow with it. (Proverbs 10:22 NKJV)* The Lord is the one that does the blessing.

God was ordering my steps, but I had to believe that He loved me and wanted me blessed. *"A man's heart plans his way, but the LORD directs his steps." (Proverbs 16:9 NKJV)* He wants a relationship with all His children. He wants us to love Him and put Him above all else. God wants obedience. *"Does the LORD delight in burnt offerings and sacrifices as much as in obeying the LORD? To obey is better than sacrifice, and to heed is better than the fat of rams. (1 Samuel 15:22 NIV)* I tithed the entire time I was in prison from the time I learned about tithing. I was not trying to waste more time. I had a lot of catching up to do after wasting so much money in my life. There were others like me that could receive this material from the seed I sowed. I wanted God to have my all. I wanted to be obedient in everything I knew.

One day Shona, another friend of mine, and me were walking the prison compound. We were having a normal walk. Shona looked at me and said, "Tressa, tell the truth when are you going home?" As soon as she asked me, the Lord spoke to me in a loud audible voice just as Shona had spoken, and said, "You shall have whatsoever you say." All I could think of is this voice I heard that I know she didn't hear. I answered her and said, "soon". I have no idea why I said that when I heard that voice. That was the first thought I had and so I spoke it. I think it was because I was so stunned of what I heard, and I knew that came from the scripture that I had been meditating on and confessing. I confessed the word so much that now the word was speaking back to me. I was dedicated. I felt that for the Lord to speak in a way that I had never heard so loud, that He was pleased with me, and He wanted to make sure I got it. I would often get up around four in the morning to pray and spend time with God before everyone in the dorm would get up. One morning the Lord told me to give all the money I had. I contemplated with that thought for about two days because in prison you never know when you will get money. It's up to people outside to decide if they will send you some money. I had $923 dollars and after going over and over in my mind, I said to myself I have to do this. I can't worry if I will get more money or not. I have to trust the Lord! *And my God shall supply all your need according to His riches in glory by Christ Jesus. (Philippians 4:19 NKJV)* I filled out the form as I normally did to send the money out to Kenneth Copeland Ministries, but this time I was called to meet with my counselor that evening. Everyone has a counselor that they were assigned. When I got the information, the counselor wanted to see me. I was like oh Lord what does she want? I went to the scheduled meeting with her, and she had me wait for twenty minutes outside her door. I went in and said, "Hi Mrs. Godwin". She asked me to sit down. She said, "Why are you sending all of your money out of the prison?" I said, "Excuse me". She said. "Why are you sending all of your money out of the prison?" I answered, "Because the Lord told me to send all my money". She said, "What did you say?" I answered again in the same respectful manner, "Because the Lord told me to send all my money." I had just received $50 dollars the day before in my account so my account would have a remaining $50 dollars. So, she asked, "well why are you sending just $923 dollars?" I said, "Because that was all the money I had when the Lord told me to send it." I had begun to tell her sometimes Mrs. Godwin we put our trust in everything but God. We put trust in our money, house, car, job, all the things that we can see, and sometimes God just wants to see us trust Him. Tears began to form in her eyes, and I had no idea why. I was just speaking to her what I knew in my own life to be true with my relationship with God. She told me she understood what I was saying. She used to spend time with God. I spoke with her about the Lord for about 30 minutes. She said at first I thought you were crazy, but after speaking with you. I am going to make sure the money is sent out today. I knew something I said connected with her.

The next day as I was leaving the cafeteria for lunch she saw me and pulled me over to the side, and said thank you. She told me the conversation we had the day before, blessed her life so much! I walked out the door, saying Lord you love your people, you would have me to give all the money away so that you could speak through me to reach one of your own. You are truly a God of love.

I was still ministering to women, and had been incarcerated approximately five years. I was still having bible study, and I stayed at the chapel every moment I could. I would listen to songs of worship, and look at preached sermons. I also worked at the dental office. The dentist wanted to see anyone that worked for him get out and do good. I had befriended another young woman name Freda. She said that she was a prophetess of god, and I never questioned anyone's relationship with God because that was not my place. She was not in my dorm, but she'd heard I had a lot of knowledge of God, and she wanted to learn. I never tried to hide any knowledge or revelation that God had given me, it was just easier to share with the ladies in my dorm or that worked with me, or that I was around the most. I tried to have bible study outside sometimes if I could because I knew others wanted to share. A few months had gone by and Freda had stopped by the dentist office to see me. She said that she had a word from god for me so I said ok. She said the Lord told her to tell me I was not going home. I had a lot of revelation knowledge that I was choosing not to share, and because of this I was not going home. I looked at her and said, "Really?" I said Freda, "I am glad that you came to me with this untruth because if it would have been another sister that was not as strong in her faith you would have destroyed her and ruined her for what she was trying to believe God for." She looked surprised as I was speaking to her so calmly and with love. I told her please don't ever do that again, I walked away and went back to work. She didn't know I had bible study every night because she was not in my dorm.

Two weeks had gone by, I was working my normal shift and the phone rang. The dentist answered the phone and he turned around and looked at me. He had a huge smile on his face as he was handing me the phone and at the same time he said, "Tressa, you are going home!" I said, "What?" as I was answering the phone. The Admin office said, "Tressa we have a fax that just came through signed off by your judge. You are immediately released from prison. We have someone coming to get you and we have thirty minutes to get you off our compound. The judge had signed my husband's papers also and reduced his sentence. I couldn't believe my ears. *The king's heart is in the hand of the LORD, as the rivers of water; He turns it wherever He wishes." (Proverbs 21:1 NKJV)*

I began to shout to the dentist, "He did it. I told you He was going to do it!" *"The Lord is not slack concerning His promise, as some count slackness, but is longsuffering toward us, not willing that any should perish but that all should come to repentance." (II Peter 3:9 NKJV)* The guard was already at the door to escort me to my dorm to get my things, as I was running down the stairs the first person I ran into was Freda. I looked and smiled, not in an arrogant way, but to let her know God moved on my faith. *"For by grace you have been saved through faith, and this is not from yourselves, it is the gift of God not by works, so that no one can boast for we are God's handiwork, created in Christ Jesus to do good works, which God prepared in advance for us to do." (Ephesians 2:8-10 NIV)* The word spread around the prison compound fast. The ladies were watching me walk through getting my stuff. I got in the car and I was out. No one was expecting me to come home. I went to my aunt's house first. She took me over my dad's house. My children were still at school, and I went to my dad's house because he was taking care of them. He was on the back porch with my uncle. When I walked on the back porch my dad thought that he had seen a ghost. He knew it was someone standing there that looked like his daughter, but he thought she was in prison. I said, "Daddy it's me. I'm home". We talked and we had already mended portions of our relationship when I was gone, as God healed me. My children finally got home. As they were getting off the bus they couldn't believe their eyes. They had heard from rumors and so many people from the beginning as children that I was never getting out. My baby boy wouldn't let me out his sight. Every time I went somewhere he was right there with me. This kid loves his mother. God was still blessing me. I had nothing of material value, and I was back at my dad's house. This time it was different. My dad enjoyed me being there and we enjoyed each other. His new wife cared for me just as much as my dad did.

Remember I said that you do not give God anything that he doesn't give back. My aunt had purchased me a car, and my husband's sister had picked me up and paid for me to get my license. I still maintained my faith, and was looking for a job. Of course, the hype was always that a person getting out of prison had a hard time finding a job. My uncle was taking me to places, and we went to the college to try and see if a lady he knew had any openings for me. As we were talking she was saying she didn't have anything, but then my uncle called me by my nickname, "Muffin". She said, "What did he call you?" I said, "Muffin". Then she came over to where I was sat down, and began to tell me that was her nickname also, and how she wanted to let me know her story. She had done prison time. She had actually done 10 years at a young age. She began to make some calls, and told one of her friends about me, and he hired me. I had a job, license and a car three days after being home. I got a promotion on the job just three weeks after being there, but after a few months I kept feeling the Lord wanted me in a town away from there. I'd known of a church family that had agreed to let me come to their town. I would often say Lord give me a church family. I found a job in that area and I moved. I knew them because this was one group of the many that would come in the jail and we stayed in contact. I often wondered why all the outsiders that came to this church would leave and not come back. I had asked one of the girls that I was in jail with to come back to that church because I was there now. She told me she wasn't coming back there, but never gave me a reason why, but I knew she was hurting. After getting there it was ok starting out, but after Church I noticed that some of them would get together, and they would gossip about others and it grieved my spirit, because I wanted to help people. Not talk about them. I honestly think that they didn't see their comments as gossip, but I saw gossip as when you talk about another person that you have no intentions to help. They were overall good people. I think that I had renewed my mind to the things of Christ so much that I was different, and if you do not continually renew your mind to the things of Christ you can be saved, but still have worldly activities, and slip back into things and think it's acceptable. This can happen to anyone if you do not constantly guard your heart to protect the things of God.

One day as I was ministering in church, I prayed a portion of the night and that morning. I felt led to speak on the revelation that God had given me where he gave me the vision of being baptized in the body of Christ. I read the word straight from the bible. They told me to get my bible and sit down, I was just a young minister, and told others not to listen to me. I went back and cried asking God why did He have me to give that word when He knew that was going to happen. I was truly hurt. As I was watching television, a minister was teaching in regards to there being no age in the Spirit. He went on to say that David was anointed King years before he sat on the throne. *"If anyone will not welcome you or listen to your words, leave that home or town and shake the dust off your feet". (Matthew 10:14 NIV)* This was a lesson to me. God's Truth is not welcomed everywhere, and that even goes for some Church buildings. Don't miss God because of your traditions.

My husband, and I decided to divorce, remain friends, and respect each other. We had been apart for quite some time, and the struggles from the past infidelity had taken its toll. We both were just young when we married and really didn't know a lot about a true unity of God. I remained single for a few years. I was working, going to church and attending college to complete my bachelor's degree in Christian Psychology. I had some friends who were constantly trying t o g e t m e connected on social media sites. I was getting friend request, and sending friend request. I connected with my middle school boyfriend. His mother had always said I was his first love. He was always a dedicated person when it concerned his relationships. My mother had passed away and his mother had told him that she'd seen me at the funeral. As we connected, we discovered we were both single. He was very respectful and caring and had positive standards for his life.

Willie and I constantly saw each other. We enjoyed each other everywhere we went. We went everywhere together - church, out to eat, the park, his mom's, my dad's and whenever you saw one you saw the other. I felt like I had life again, and really enjoyed myself with him. He was my best friend and we talked about everything. We laughed, joked, played. We talked about the old school days and just had a good time laughing and being around each other. We were just right for each other. Every day I found myself thanking God for him. The manifestation of the blessing was being seen in my life and continued.

Willie desired to be with me and only me. I had abundance of joy and peace. We have been together loving each other every since. God has blessed me with his best that pertains to my life. Each day in prayer I give thanks to God for my loving, supportive husband Willie Mitchener Jr. God knew what I needed.

Then devastation hit our family. One of my nephews was killed in a tragic car accident. This was a significantly heart breaking time for us. We just couldn't understand why; he was so young, and vibrant. At one point, all of our kids grew up together and the boys were just like brothers, so to lose one just wasn't fair. I encouraged my brother that God was faithful even when we don't understand. I knew that my nephew had been emotionally tore up from an experience just a few months prior where his girlfriend was hit by a car and passed away. This conversation led him and I to talk about God. I was able to answer a few questions about the bible, which gave him peace, and now he was gone. I had applied for a job at a large Heating and Air company, and I didn't get the job. In our crisis, I was there to support my brother, and anyone else that I could to help get through this. I saw the owner and his wife at my brother's house. My brother worked for the company. When everyone was trying to comfort each other, and help out however they could, I went outside on the porch doing the only thing I knew to do, give God's word, and minister His Grace, because He is the God of all comfort. *"Blessed be the God and Father of our Lord Jesus Christ, the father of mercies and God of all comfort."* *(II Corinthians 1:3 NKJV)* I started speaking with the owner's wife and my cousin telling them what I knew about God, His love, and His great covenant. I was explaining that God loves us and has graced us. I wanted to remind them that God is faithful in spite of what we all were suffering. They were moved to tears. Somehow I ended up talking to the owner, and he told me to come to the company and apply for the job. This was over a year after the first time I applied. I got the job and moved up quickly. I was incredibly impressed with how the owner was so compassionate for others and how he had an energy that thrived off of seeing others succeed.

God has blessed me on many occasions with His favor. *"And so find favor and high esteem in the sight of God and Man"* *(Proverbs 3:4 NKJV)* My husband and I have been blessed to build two homes together. *"When the Lord your God brings you into the land he swore to your fathers, to Abraham,*

Isaac, and Jacob, to give you a land with large, flourishing

cities, you did not build, houses filled with all kinds of good things

you did not provide, wells you did not dig, and vineyards and

olive groves you did not plant then when you eat and are

satisfied" (Deuteronomy 6:10:11 NIV) God restored my life in spite of everyone that didn't believe. I had said for years that *I would trust him.* It was those words that I spoke at the beginning, **_'I will trust and believe God'._**

I did see my sons' father when I got home, and I wasn't upset with him. I wasn't upset with anyone. I loved everyone. I began to talk to him about the Lord, and asked him would he like to accept the Lord as his savior. He said yes and I went through the salvation prayer with him. I had an extra bible and I gave it to him. A little while after I had been home he ended up back in prison, and never made it out. He was beat to death in his cell by four guys that came into his cell in the middle of the night. When his sister and I rode out together. She held up the bible I had given him, and told me before he had gone to prison that he did read it. I am blessed to know that in spite of anything that he did he asked the Lord to be his savior before this. God doesn't rate sin.

He said that he would forgive us for all our sin if we confessed and believe on him.

My mother passed away 6 months prior to his death, and once again, I am grateful to say when she came to visit me in prison I ministered to her and she told me that she knew what I was saying about Jesus Christ was true and she wanted to be saved. She just couldn't understand the amazing transformation that had happened to me. I was so fluent in the knowledge of God's word. It was if I had adopted another language because Christ was all I had to talk about. I asked her did she want to be saved. She sat there with tears rolling down her face and shook her head yes. I said let's do it momma! I led her to Christ. My mother did get to see me teach God's word in church before her death. I saw her on the back pew crying the whole time. When we were on the way home she was amazed. God answered my prayer; my mother got to see me do life the right way. My prayer was that my family be saved, but in the midst of everyone dying, I realized that I had become the answer to my own prayer that I had prayed. I had the opportunity to witness to them hand in hand with mine as they asked the Lord to come into their life. "I *planted, Apollos watered, but God gave the increase. So then neither he who plants is anything, nor he who waters, but God who gives the increase." (I Corinthians 3:6-7 NKJV)* God shows that He works through many in order to get a prayer answered. Do not miss your call or opportunity to bless someone. I pray that this book answers many prayers because I have been where many of you may be or have been.

I have been a rebellious teen, teenage mom, without the support of a parent, feeling not wanted, physically abused, broke, lonely, without hope, spiritually blind, being cheated on, having my own adulterous relationship, in jail, in prison, but all I can say now is: **"BUT GOD"** *who was on my side. Without him where would I be?* He made all things new.

You may be asking God to answer prayers for you, but you may just need to look in the mirror. You may be your answer. I had all of my family and anyone that may have been an enemy on a list I prayed for them every day. I loved everyone and had no bitterness in my heart towards anyone. I just wanted to love them, as Christ loved me. I prayed for everyone because I wanted everyone set free, and for the enemy to have no power over them. I still have my list with many names on it to this day to take before the Lord each morning. My dad, my brother, and me are enjoying our relationship together. We spend as much time as we can together, along with my dad's wife. She enjoys it. She cook us all our favorite foods that we may be blessed eating together. My brother and I have tried to arrange occasions to spend time with all our family and friends because that's what it's all about, others. My brother and I are still there for each other no matter what. My mother and father in law also love me as their very own daughter and will do anything for me. This book is to let everyone know the power of forgiveness and the love that allowed a second chance. God loves us all, and desires that we all be saved, and blessed. Do not allow this life to pass you by without doing God's will for your life. You have to reach back and tell others of the hope that brought you out and helped you. How did you overcome? Give God his Glory. *"And they overcame him by the blood of the Lamb, and by the word of their testimony, and they did not love their lives to the death." (Revelation 12:11 NKJV).*

You have to say yes to what is on the inside.

You have eyes to see on the inside and ears to hear on the inside. When you dream, you can see, but your eyes are closed, and when you read you can hear without mumbling a w o r d on the paper. God didn't' make you this way for no reason. He gave you tools to life on the inside to help you hear him direct your path. Learn to live from on the inside this is how the Spirit will lead your path. He is not counting wrongs. He just wants you in his loving arms of relationship daily. Don't ever think that you have to try and get it right first to come to God. If that was the case he died for nothing. He died because he knew we couldn't do it on our own and we needed a savior. God himself left the throne and wrapped himself in flesh as a man Jesus Christ and handled his business. He gave one son so that now he may have many sons and daughters. He did it for me and for you!

<u>Salvation Prayer</u>

Dear Heavenly father, I ask you to come live in my heart. I come to you in the name of Jesus. You said if I confess with my mouth "Jesus Is Lord," and I believe in my heart that God raised him from the dead. I shall be saved. For with the heart man believe unto righteousness and with the mouth confession is made unto salvation. It is with your heart that you believe and are justified, and it is with your mouth that you confess and are saved (Romans 10:9,10 NIV). Start reading and applying the word to your life.

ABOUT THE AUTHOR

Tressa Mitchener is a wife, mother of two sons, one daughter, a grandmother to three. She has used her voice to educate and empower people through the word of God, after making all the wrong choices during a world filled with spiritual darkness. With her countless life challenges and the struggle of her own spiritual blindness, she emerged with spiritual vision, filled with the Holy Spirit, and the anointing of God, with new eyesight and a message in her mouth!

This anointed woman of God stands as a powerful teacher and Christian life coach. Helping many, has afforded her the opportunity to cross both cultural, denominational and international lines due to her masterful relevant approach to bring the message of Jesus Christ redemptive power.

Tressa fulfilled a great accomplishment in obtaining

a Bachelor's degree in Psychology & Christian Counseling and is currently pursuing her Master's Degree in Christian Ministries & Life Coaching. She is equipped and studies the word of God to show herself approved, rightfully dividing the word of Truth. Tressa is the CEO and founder of REVAMP: Tressa Mitchener Inc., dedicated to help others gain a new and improved appearance, structure and form for every area of their life. Reaching your potential and purpose for others and yourself. Working together to accomplish a common goal. Believing in yourself and others.

To invite Tressa for a speaking engagement at your church, business or nonprofit organization, to tell her riveting life story, or to purchase additional copies of "Looking Out From The Inside", feel free to contact her at:

www.tressamitchener.me

Tressa Mitchener
PO Box 1983
Clayton, NC 27528
919-207-0002

Made in the USA
Charleston, SC
06 March 2017